List Building Lifestyle

Confessions of an Email Millionaire

Igor Kheifets

List Building Lifestyle

Independently Published

Copyright © 2019, Igor Kheifets

Published in the United States of America

ISBN: 9781099914492
181205-01247-3

Praise for Igor Kheifets

"Igor's quickly risen to become one of the greatest list builders I've ever met. If you're looking to build a list, he's the perfect addition to your team."

Matt Bacak, founder, EPC Institute

"Igor's one of the top email marketers I know, and he is relentless about his client's success. If you want to make money with email marketing, he's your man."

Craig Ballantyne, author, The Perfect Day Formula

"Some walk the talk, others dominate it. That's Igor."

Steve Sims, author, Bluefishing

"Seize every opportunity to work with Igor. He's one of the guys in list building. I've made $20,000 in one week working with him."

Ron Douglas, New York Times Best Selling Author, America's Most Wanted Recipes

Is List Building Lifestyle Right For You?

If you've picked up a copy of this book, there are a few things I know about you. You feel trapped. You're overwhelmed. You don't know what you're supposed to do next to grow your income and your personal freedom. You're looking for the fastest way to create a purposeful life where you can help people, be free, and make a lot of money.

If that's you, you picked up the right book, because the fastest way to make a lot, contribute a lot to other people's lives and enjoy lots of free time is to build your own email list of people who like you and trust you in a passionate niche market. I explain how to do that in the following chapters.

If, however, you're just looking for a stable paycheck, if you love your job, if you're fine with cruising through meaningless grey existence lacking purpose, excitement and freedom to do what you want, when you want, with whom you want, List Building Lifestyle offers no value to you.

I invite you to get excited to discover how to join the new economy as a producer, rather than a consumer. Let me walk you through the mechanics of how average people with no previous experience are out earning lawyers, dentists, doctors and stock brokers working from their kitchen table. Get ready to discover the List Building Lifestyle.

Here's What's Inside...

Foreword

Email is not dead. Email is not dying. Email is the Internet's version of looking into the mirror naked. It tells you the truth about your business, unlike social media where you can get caught up in the likes, loves, and shares, thinking that you're making progress just because you see a few hearts on the screen. But you cannot deposit any of those into the bank. And 99% of social media marketers have no idea how to make the big leap from a "like" to a dollar bill.

That's not the case with email. If you have an email list, you pretty much have an ATM connected to your computer. And as long as you follow what Igor teaches you in this book, you'll know how to turn those emails into money in your bank account. Even in today's world of shiny social medial bells and whistles, email is the simplest form of automating your income.

I built my first email list in 1999 and was making money online before I graduated with my Master's Degree in Exercise Physiology (which was not nearly as useful as my self-taught Ph.D. in email marketing). In the past 20 years I've watched hundreds of Internet Marketing trends come and go, but email has passed the test of time. And if a naïve, newbie farm boy like myself could make money with email since the turn of last century, then you'll be able to "press send and make money" well into this new millennium.

Email marketing can become your primary lead source. It can deliver constant cash flow. It *can* make you money while you sleep. It is the Holy Grail of Internet Marketing and you cannot ignore it. It allowed me to reach thousands of people while sending messages from my college's computer lab, even before I had a computer of my own – let alone an Internet connection at home. Today it allows me to generate consistent cash flow from anywhere in the world and it supports my Empire of multiple 7-figure businesses, and it can do the same for you.

That's how it goes with email. Igor knows this. I know this. My mentor best-selling author of "Ready, Fire, Aim" Michael Masterson and the billion-dollar company he consults, Agora, knows this. My friend Joel Marion who has sold over $500,000,000 worth of supplements and information products through email knows this. There is no substitute – not FB chat, not IG DM's, not comments on YouTube... definitely not comments on YouTube, where you'd find yourself arguing with a 14-year old. Most successful marketers live by their email list, and you need to pay attention to this gold mine of an opportunity.

Follow the treasure map Igor reveals in this book, and then enjoy the freedom, the luxury lifestyle (or the simple, hassle-free lifestyle of a modern-day minimalist), and income automation that email marketing delivers.

Whatever life you desire and deserve, having an email list of people who like you and trust you and who want to buy from you – with Igor's help – will give it to you.

Craig Ballantyne
Owner, EarlyToRise
Author, *Perfect Day Formula*

Introduction

What's the most precious commodity of the 21st century? Some will argue it is gold because it comes in short supply and is hard to find. Forward-thinking futurists will tell you it is water because we're running out. You can probably guess oil is valuable too because we're burning through 86 million barrels of crude oil a day and there are only 1.7 billion of it left in reserve. While all the above are valuable, none are as valuable as *our attention*. World's most precious commodity can't be mined, poured into a glass, or used to fuel your Volvo. Yet, it can make you very rich very fast.

Attention monetization has been world's most profitable companies' #1 priority for nearly two decades. Google earns billions annually selling attention and intent. Facebook is coming up with new ways to keep people scrolling through the feed on a weekly basis. Besides leading the field in the art of keeping you glued to your smartphone, Mark Zuckerberg has also made it a mission to absorb every start-up that's getting high engagement from its users. In recent years, Facebook acquired Instagram and WhatsApp for astronomical figures. Did they buy it for the software? No. Not in a million years. Facebook bought the *eyeballs*. That's where the money is, and Facebook knows it.

Welcome to the new economy, an economy that doesn't reward skilled workers or even the hard-working entrepreneur. Welcome to the world where a 17-year-old kid who is reviewing video games on YouTube, out-earns lawyers, doctors, and stockbrokers in their underwear. It is an economy where celebrities are created with the ease of the "go live" button, an economy where being visible is more profitable than being valuable, helpful, or skillful.

I bring up Facebook and Google to make a point: money is attracted to those who can capture and monetize viewer's attention. The rest of this book is not going to be about social media or search engines. I won't try to convince you to become the next Gary Vee. In fact, my message is very different from most "internet marketing" books sitting on the shelf next to this one. I'm going to open your eyes to lead generation beyond social media and Google. I'm going to show you a traffic source twenty times more profitable than social networks. By the time you're done reading this book, you'll know exactly how to get hundreds of new leads per day on complete autopilot.

I wrote this book for people who want to grow their freedom while growing their income. I'm going to introduce you to a "secret society" of lazy millionaires who make more money before breakfast than most people make per month. You're going to see how to break the link between your time and your income using a strategy called *List Building*. My goal is to help you see and understand how you can make money in any economy with permission-based email marketing. You're going to see how average people create fortunes sending out emails to small groups of people who happily pay them $97, $1,997, and even $4,997 without ever talking to them or meeting them in person. I'm excited to introduce you to an online business that can support any lifestyle you choose. The best part is, you don't even need to hire employees, buy a franchise, or even rent a location.

I promise, if you follow the strategies shared in this book, you'll be able to make more in the next 12 months than in the previous 12 years. Excited? Then flip the page and let's get going.

To Your List Building Lifestyle,

Igor Kheifets

Chapter 1
You – The Next Email Millionaire?

I'm an average guy. I don't own any Ferraris, and I don't fly private jets. When I walk down the street, people don't recognize me. They don't know my name, and they don't approach me for an autograph. But I have what most people don't. I am a free man.

I have financial freedom. I have location freedom, and I have freedom of choice. I don't have to put up with anything I don't want to in my life. I don't have to put up with a boss. I don't have to put up with people I don't like. I don't have to put up with circumstances I don't like. I don't have to live my life according to other people's standards. I don't have to put up with a job I'm not passionate about. I come and go as I please. I don't have an office, and I can live and work out anywhere in the world.

My average day looks something like this. I wake up around 7:45 a.m., I brush my teeth and go downstairs. I make scrambled eggs for my daughter, Erica, while my wife feeds, Chris, our little one. I get dressed, pack Erica's snack box, and drive her to school. Having dropped her off at school, I drive to the Landwer Coffee Shop on Bathurst Street, where I'll spend the next four hours "working."

Work means checking my earnings, traffic statistics and email open rates. Next, I answer emails from my team and private clients. After that I give instructions to my team of remote freelancers and contractors on what needs to be done that week and plan for the rest of the month, making sure everyone is on track to hit their targets.

I do all of this while having my first and second, then my, third, and fourth espressos. I'm pretty big on espresso. I think I'm addicted. Working out of coffee shops most of the time doesn't help, I guess. Coffee is my 2nd addiction. My work is my first. Even though I don't physically work 24/7, I still think, for the most part, about marketing stuff on the internet all day long.

Why do I choose to work in coffee shops? There are two reasons. First off, I love the aroma. It smells better than any office I've ever worked in. Second, it doesn't feel like a real job. And that's very important to me. The moment it does – it's no fun anymore. I've tried working in all kinds of different shared office spaces, like WeWork and places like that. It didn't work for me because within a week; I felt like I'd signed up for a job. I really hated that.

I follow the exact same routine no matter the city I'm visiting that week. I've done it in London, Munich, Berlin, Amsterdam, Manchester, Paris, Orlando, Las Vegas, Dallas, Toronto, Moscow, St. Petersburg, San Diego, Los Angeles and a bunch of other places. It didn't matter if I was there on business or just site seeing. It didn't matter if I was there on my own, with friends, or with family. I could always carve out four hours in the morning to do what's necessary in order to keep the money coming in, and then go about my life any way I want.

But my life wasn't always sunshine and rainbows. At one point it sucked. *Really-really* sucked. I'm sharing how I turned it around in the following pages. Good news for you, my success wasn't accidental. I went from worrying about where "today money" is going to come from to having systems that bring in new customers and new business for my company automatically every minute of every day including weekends and holidays. I sincerely believe anyone who wants to get rich online needs to know what I know. How can I be so sure my system will work for you? Because I found a way to break the link between my income and my time as well as my location and my health.

This online success system, if you will, is universal. It doesn't discriminate against your background, age or gender. I taught it to thousands of people. You may be wondering, why teach my system to others, if I've already got my life set?

Two reasons. First, because in spite of a large amount of information, books, courses and so-called expert workshops available these days – working from home is still a subject of much confusion. I've developed a clear and simple approach to starting and scaling a highly-profitable internet business with low costs and low time investment. My method eliminates unnecessary moving parts. It speeds up your results. It doesn't require an MBA.

Second, because money has become the corner stone of our day to day life. Your income determines the quality of every aspect of your life; especially your family life. I wrote this book for people who want to give their families the life they deserve, just like my mom and dad tried to do it for me and my older brother, Oleg.

I'll always remember my dad. He worked hard when I was a kid. He graduated the Moscow Suvorov Military School a Red Army Lieutenant long before the iron curtain came crashing down in 1991. He was dispatched to Ukraine where my brother and I were eventually born. Later, he got discharged and started a shashlik kiosk. Soon he had 3 locations and a ton of stress. His 14 hour work days combined with alcohol lead to a heart attack and another a year later. He spent weeks in the hospital under observation without being able to work to provide for us.

Imagine me, 8, and my brother 17, and my mom who hadn't had a job in years borrowing money from friends and family to buy bread and milk while our family's breadwinner is recovering after 2 massive heart attacks. Most women didn't work back in the 90s in the Ukraine. That was the social model everyone abided by. Women were supposed to stay home and raise the kids. The man was the provider. At that point in time we had no provider. My mom was petrified. This experience planted the seed in my mind. Eventually it has outgrown every other desire I've ever had.

All I wanted was two things; a family of my own. And to be really-really rich, so my family never had to go through what I went through as a child. I didn't want my income to depend on my location, my health, my free time (or lack of thereof) and my actual work hours. I wanted total and complete control over my life.

Before I would become one of the world's top email marketers, I'd go through a journey full of trials and tribulations. I share some of those and the lessons they taught me in this book.

I worked quite a few "starter jobs." I scrubbed toilets in a 4-star hotel. I washed dishes and mopped floors at Burger King. I did it all. After working 8, 10, 12 hours a day, at the end of the month, I got paid next to nothing. I remember getting my statement one time showing I've worked 307 hours that month. I was saving up to buy a laptop and I worked really hard to make it happen. But even after putting all these hours, I was still $200 short at the end of the month. I was like, "Yeah, I don't see how I can get rich this way, so let's go look for another way." That is when I jumped into internet marketing.

I consider myself very fortunate because I've got more customers wanting to work with me than I can handle these days. And anytime I run out of new clients, I'm just one email away from a stampede of hungry buyers to my doorstep. I don't share this to brag, but help you see and understand the secret to my success.

Douglas MacArthur famously said "security lies in our ability to produce." To paraphrase the five-star general, "financial security lies in our ability to produce new customers and sales on demand." Nothing gives higher sense of security than the certainty of knowing you can send out an email and watch your bank account instantly fill with money. Today, this is much easier done than in the pre-internet era, where the only people who made a lot of money and reached tons of people were the ones who could secure a late night TV slot. Think of someone like, Tony Robbins, who had the famous Guthy|Renker infomercial that turned him into an overnight phenomenon. If you look at the marketplace today, you'll see that Tony Robbins is no different from 123,221 other gurus who market in the exact same way, teach the same content, conduct similar seminars and charge similar prices. The internet has leveled the playing field. Now you and I can make just as large of an impact as the so-called gurus (No disrespect to Tony, by the way. I love the guy. He changed my life!).

Your background doesn't matter. Your connections don't matter. Your age, your gender, your ethnicity – don't matter. Maybe you're a high-paid executive tired of her stressful job. Or perhaps you're an Uber driver who recently immigrated who struggles to pay the bills. Whoever you are, the internet offers you an opportunity to live life on your own terms.

You can start a multi-million-dollar business out of a 1-bedroom studio apartment in New York just as easily as you can build a thriving home business out of your momma's back yard deck. I started my business out of my bedroom in a 3-room apartment located in a duplex on the south end of a hick town deep in the south east Israel. I created my own economy in a town with no economy. Just like my mom and dad, most people who lived in my home town worked for the only corporation that offered jobs. When the company went bankrupt half the town was left without an income. 2/3rds left. 1/3rd stayed to collect social security.

Here's what this means for you: your time is now. Your dream business is within reach. I must warn you, though, my strategies do not involve you becoming a social media celebrity. They're not based on feel-good theory. I'm not going to be showing you how to ride trends or how to suck up to Google so it dispenses a few clicks your way. You'll find none of that here, because I tried it all and it didn't work. Instead, I'd like to share with you the *one* thing that worked for me and my many students.

My method is based on measurable and predictable traffic strategy which delivers immediate results when applied correctly. The rest of this book is going to be about answering questions such as: How do I get lots and lots of buyer traffic? How do I turn this traffic into customers? How do I get the eyeballs, and how do I turn the eyeballs into leads and customers who want to give me money? What do I need to start and scale a 6-figure online business? How to find products to promote if I don't have money to manufacture products or any creative ideas? How to use email marketing to create your own economy no matter where you are in the world and many other questions on your mind right now.

You will find the rest of this book fascinating if the idea of trying to get rich in your local economy doesn't make sense to you. I grew up in a small town with a shrinking local economy. Where I come from, people don't think in terms of getting rich. They're trying to get by. Most are mooching the government for financial aid. This book goes against this type of thinking. I wrote this book for those who want more. More money. More freedom. More lifestyle. More impact. More contribution. More experiences. More opportunities.

No matter your background, your current income, your upbringing or your resources, this book is going to show you how to get rich using the internet. It will open your eyes to a brand new economy and give you a step-by-step playbook to win in it. It is my hope this book inspires you to see and understand how to become the next email millionaire.

Chapter 2
True Cost of Free Traffic

When I first found out I could earn money from home, I rejected it, because it seemed too good to be true. I thought I was being rational. Now I know I was just being narrow-minded. Growing up surrounded by poverty and lack, I never knew another way of thinking.

I attended a military academy between the ages of 14 and 19. The academy specialized in engineering and microchips. I've been taught to be pragmatic and over-analyze everything – the opposite of what natural entrepreneurs tend to do. I was very much "inside the box" thinker and doer. I wasn't very ambitious either. I never dreamed of making millions of dollars a year. I was happy just to get a job.

This whole world of making money from home didn't even seem real to me. Admitting such possibility was real would be to admit my entire life was one big waste of effort. Buying into this idea would mean everything I was told about what's right was in fact wrong. This isn't uncommon way of thinking. One of the most common things you'll see online is people who've been flirting with the idea of starting a home based business but never fully committing to it. In fact, many people, even after they start making money online, continue holding on to their day job, because they're afraid their online business is temporary stroke of luck at best.

This irrational fear stems from limited understanding of what internet marketing is. Imagine you're 30 feet deep under water exploring the wonders of the sea. Suddenly, you spot a mean-looking shark heading your way. It's accelerating and its jaws are wide open getting ready to pierce you with two rows of razor-sharp teeth. If you're an inexperienced diver or if you know nothing about sharks, you've already seen your life flash before your eyes. If, however, you're a skilled aquanaut, you didn't even notice the predator, because you know this is a basking shark that only eats plankton. Knowing what you're dealing with makes a difference in your critical thinking.

In many ways internet marketing is the basking shark of the economy. People who first come across this amazing industry, due to lack of knowledge about it, refuse to believe it is real. But it is. Frankly, they've got no idea what they're saying "no" to. The moment I embraced internet marketing was when I understood the money-making process. At first, I thought money magically manifests on the internet through clicking links and filling out surveys. Unfortunately, it's a little bit more complicated than that. Incidentally, making money on the internet is not much different than making money offline. Just like offline, you still need a product, a place to showcase your product and the consumers to sell it to.

The only difference is, unless you're into Amazon drop shipping, the internet allows you to market non-tangible (digital) products and services that don't require a physical location, a store, a warehouse or anything other than a website (and sometimes not even that).

Would you like a completely "done for you" digital business? Visit www.igor.cx/tools for the up-to-date list of Igor's recommended "business in a box" opportunities.

Before you laugh at the premise of strangers sending you money over the internet for products they can't eat, touch, smell or wear, think of all the non-tangible products you bought in the past. Products such as consulting, coaching, access to forums, membership sites with content, masterminds and a bunch of other stuff you can't even remember now. Yes, this is a real industry. And it's pretty big. According to research (which I would totally back up with a study conducted by some dude with 5 letters after his name if anyone cared), it's a $160B industry. I may not have my numbers right on this one, but trust me – there's a lot of money here and it's easy to collect your share if you know the rules of engagement.

Here's how to make money online. Internet marketing is a *business of making compelling offers to hungry* audiences. To make money, you need two things: *a great offer* and *targeted audience* (aka traffic). When you successfully combine these two components, you create conversions. And conversions equal money in the bank.

Since I didn't know how to build my own offer, create my own product, build my own website or do anything "internetsy" other than instant message my friends on ICQ (yeah, I'm old!), I started by promoting a $10 MLM (multi-level-marketing) opportunity. The lady, who referred me to this opportunity, didn't even have to sell me. She just sent me a 12 minute video (aka video sales letter or VSL for short) that did all the selling for her. The video said, "Refer your friend, and your friend refers two friends, and then, those friends refer two friends each and before you know it, you'll be making $3,000 per month in passive income."

I was like, "Wow! That sounds easy. I can do that. I can bring nine people, who bring nine people, who bring nine people and I'll be a millionaire in 30 days!" I quickly discovered it's not going to be a walk in the park. I tried singing up my mom and my best friend Max. My mom said no. Max signed up for a $1 trial and cancelled the next day. I hated being rejected. I took every "no" personally.

My upline suggested I try my luck online. At least, I wouldn't have to talk to people. This is when I first learned about traffic. I still couldn't tell between high-quality traffic and low-quality traffic. I was just trying to get some eye balls on my affiliate link.

I was broke. I couldn't afford to buy traffic. So I've done what every forum and blog post suggested I'd do – social media. I started building Facebook profiles and Twitter profiles trying to siphon some traffic from social media sites. Within a few days I've had dozens of fake profiles with a fake rags to riches story and everything. Then I started adding 50 friends a day to build traffic. The idea was to have these people look into my profile, find my story inspiring and click on my affiliate link.

Did it work? Nope. The only thing it did was put me in Facebook jail a lot. I thought, "Okay that's not the best use of my time. Let me try automating this process, because if I could create more profiles and add more friends in less time, I may squeeze some money out of the internet after all." I bought software to automatically create Twitter profiles. Once it created the profile with the parameters I set, the Twitter bot would follow thousands of people every day. The idea was to trigger a sense of reciprocity and have all these people follow me back.

Not much changed since I attempted this Twitter approach. Many Twitter marketers still try to drive engagement this way. It was also adopted into Instagram marketing, Snapchat marketing and dozens of other social media platforms.

Refer to the "Free List Building Resources" section to find out how I generate 500 buyer leads per day on autopilot.

I built a Twitter profile with 20,000 followers this way. It seemed like a lot. Even if I only got $1 from each one of the 20,000 followers per month, I'd make $20,000 a month. Another bubble burst. I didn't make $20,000 per month. I didn't even make $20. My tweets didn't get much engagement. Eventually I quit Twitter.

Then I started researching more about free traffic, and I found article marketing. I'm not sure if you've ever done article marketing, but it involves a lot of writing. At the time, I was only 18 or 19 years old. I'd never written anything in my life, and I'm also not a native English speaker. My vocabulary was very limited. I spoke "Borat English" at best. Nevertheless, I wrote about a thousand articles that year about things related to network marketing, success and personal development. Topics any ambitious person would be interested in.

I posted my work on article directories like Ezine Articles. Google loved Ezine Articles. The idea was to rank my articles on the 1st page of Google by using the authority Ezine Articles had with Google. Same as before, I didn't get much traffic. The traffic I did get – sucked. Other than earning a "Expert Author" badge next to my profile icon, writing articles didn't do much for me.

Next I decided to start my own blog. I figured I was already writing tons of articles. Why not post these articles on my own website to build credibility and attract readers. So I built a blog. I bought a WordPress theme for $500 and I figured out the plugins I needed to optimize it. I've done some basic HTML editing to customize it. I figured out how to track my bounce rates and average time reader spent on my site. I put another eight months into that. Result? I was finally getting traffic. The Gods of traffic heard my prayers, recognized the hard work I've done and rewarded me with a trickle of visitors.

At some point I was getting about 200 visitors per day. I was happy be finally getting eyeballs. I knew money would follow soon. After a few months of getting substantial traffic, my earnings weren't growing. I looked into my Google Analytics and saw my visitors were spending roughly 15 seconds on my site on average. Less than 10% visited my blog more than once. My traffic wasn't targeted. It wasn't sticking. It wasn't buying. Another dead end.

Another 8 months down the drain. It was becoming hard to ignore the obvious – free traffic wasn't scalable. It gave me no sense of control. The few free clicks I managed to generate to my links almost never converted. And those that did convert – I couldn't scale. I wanted traffic I could control. I wanted a lead generation thermostat I could turn up and down whenever I wanted.

There's no such thing as free traffic. You either pay with your time or your money. If I took all the money I made from free traffic (minus the money I spent on software, coaching, mentoring and tools to learn how to get it) and divided it by the amount of hours I put it, my hourly pay would be roughly 1/10th of that of a McDonalds bus boy.

The so-called free traffic almost cost me my relationship. At the time I was dating my bride-to-be Anastasiya. We were living with my parents. She worked full time. I worked full time on my online business. I remember working particularly hard on a content-rich free traffic campaign. It was Anastasiya's day off and she was hoping to spend it together at the beach. I cancelled the trip to stay home and work on my business. She decided to stay home and watch TV. Later that night, I was exhausted and ready for some downtime. I came out of my room and looked for Anastasiya around the apartment. She was nowhere to be found. I called her cell. No answer. I texted her. Nothing.

After a few hours of waiting, I knew something wasn't right. I called her mom. Turned out, Anastasiya got tired of always being second to my online business. She decided to move back with her mother. I realized what I've done. Got into my dad's car and drove to her mom's house. With my tail between my legs I apologized profusely and convinced her to come back.

I'm a fast learner. Once I burn my hand on the stove – I don't touch it anymore. All the evidence was pointing to the fact I had to find another way of building my online business. I had to try a different traffic approach. Something I never tried before – I had to start paying for those damn clicks!

Chapter 3
How I Turned My Annual Income
Into My Monthly Income

Reason most internet marketers avoid paid traffic is perceived cost of failure. If a free traffic campaign fails – no harm done. You lost some time. But at least you didn't lose money. If a paid traffic campaign bombs – it hurts financially.

As we discussed earlier, there's a cost to both. And in my humble yet accurate opinion, the cost of free is far greater than dollars and cents you risk with paid traffic. On the other hand, the advantages of paid traffic outweigh the risks.

Generating leads through paid traffic is a lot like buying produce in your local superstore as opposed to growing it in your back yard. It's fast. It's easy. It doesn't require farming skills, farming equipment, soil, watering or planting. Want to make a salad? Easy. Pick the ingredients you need, pay at the register and be on your way.

Okay. Maybe it's not as simplistic as I describe it. You still need to know how to tell ripe bananas from unripe ones. Also, there's a slight chance of pesticides. Overall though, it beats growing veggies in your own backyard.

When I got into paid traffic, I still didn't see it that way. I still saw it as a mean scary monster out to eat my money. But in the absence of better options, I was willing to give it a shot.

I had to start somewhere. I chose pay-per-view traffic. You know how some people download screensavers and all kinds of adware and toolbars? Well, when they do, the PPV networks pop ads on their computers when they visit websites advertisers bid on. For example, if I was marketing exercise equipment, I would bid to pop my ad to anyone who visits Men's Health website. I would get charged a fraction of a cent per view when my ad was viewed by the consumer. This made way more sense than writing articles with no guarantee of results.

To run PPV traffic, I had to put down a $200 ad budget upfront. At the time, I was a full-time housekeeper in a 3-star hotel. I was cleaning hotel rooms and scrubbing public bathrooms spotless. I made 780-something dollars a month working 14-hour work days. $200 was a lot of money. In good conscience I couldn't invest without getting approval from Anastasiya.

She was in the living room, watching TV. I said, "Honey, I want to put 200 bucks on a traffic campaign." She looked at me in silence. I thought, "Crap. I'm losing her."

My wife isn't technical. Unless it is something you can wear, eat or put a battery in – it's not real. If I started getting technical with her, I knew exactly the response I would get.

I said, "Imagine I own a china store. I need customers to walk in to my store to buy china, right? Well, I can rent a location in a high-traffic area, so I can get lots of foot traffic. I can put up a billboard on the highway. I can buy an ad in the paper. I can start handing out flyers in the streets and so on." She replied, "Okay, yeah." I continued, "Well, I want to put up a billboard in front of the people who are already looking for china and it will pop up in front of them only when they're visiting websites that either talk about or sell china." She said agreed. I couldn't believe it. I hurried to submit the deposit before she changed her mind.

My victory was short-lived, because I burned through $200 within a day. I generated tons of visitors to my website, but I didn't make any money. It hurt like hell at the time. A week's worth of hard work down the drain. But now it seems like an inexpensive lesson that paid big dividends over the years. I knew the traffic I was getting was decent. I just wasn't working it correctly.

Over the course of the following year I've made several adjustments to my strategy. These adjustments allowed me to start seeing 30%, 50% and sometimes even 70% of my money back the same day I ran the traffic. From there, I scaled my business very-very quickly. Within just 6 months I was already closing on $10,000 per month. Within a year I hit $20,000 a month. For the first time ever I felt in control of my life, because I controlled my income through traffic.

It was the first time I felt I was finally out of the rat race. I broke the link between my time and my money. Now my income was scalable regardless of the hours I worked. I learned how to build systems that grew my income. I was still having trouble adjusting to the new reality. I was making per month working just a couple of hours a day what my mom was making working full time at a microchip facility *per year*.

Seeing all the money we were now making, Anastasiya and I decided to go on vacation to Prague. It's a place we always wanted to visit. We spent three days site seeing and drinking hot wine. I particularly remember the anxiety over not working and the fear of losing my business because I wasn't physically at the computer, managing it. And I remember how relieved I was every time we got back to the hotel, because my stats showed I was $100, $300 or even $500 richer. More... I knew exactly how to scale my business when I wanted to.

But that would come later. I still had a lot to learn about creating my List Building Lifestyle. The first thing I would need to figure out was how to convert the traffic I was getting into sales.

Would you like a step-by-step blueprint to starting, growing and automating your own six-figure online business? Visit www.igor.cx/tools for details

Chapter 4
The Big Traffic Secret No One Wants You To Know

By the time I got into paid traffic, I lost passion for network marketing. I got tired of constant rejection, regulations (promote this way and not that way) and the square-thinking most MLM companies and leaders confined their members to.

The challenge with MLM (aside from people refusing to work with you because they're not into pyramid schemes) was retention. I've had limited success with network marketing programs. In my entire life, I recruited less than a dozen people. But even at that level I saw a huge problem – retention. People were leaving faster than I could recruit them. When you're marketing a monthly subscription product, your income depends on how long people keep using it. I discovered it was harder to keep people from leaving than recruiting them and walked away.

The biggest advantage network marketing offered to someone like me, and the only reason I signed up in the first place, is not having to build my own product, get my own merchant processing or printing brochures show casing my product. MLM companies conveniently provided all the products and tools you need to run a business. That part of MLM I liked very much. I didn't want to give it up.

That's why I switched to affiliate marketing. It offered the same benefits as MLM did minus the headache of keeping customers from cancelling. I was no longer limited to one type of product or niche. I could promote software that paid 30% monthly commission just as easily as coaching program that paid 75% commission. Sometimes I promoted both at the same time to the same customers, because the products complemented each other.

There were tens of thousands of products for me to choose from. Low ticket, high ticket, mid ticket. Services, information, WordPress plugins, books. I could profit in any niche or industry without being an expert – because I promoted other experts who went through the trouble of creating, packaging and selling their own products.

As an affiliate, my job was to get targeted eyeballs to my affiliate link. If the traffic I was referring converted into sales, I would get the lion's share of the profits. If not, I didn't make money. My income was directly proportionate to the quality and the quantity of the traffic I could channel to my affiliate links.

To help incentivize their affiliates, product creators run affiliate competitions. Typically, they show case a leaderboard showcasing who has made most sales in a given week or month. Incidentally, after promoting affiliate products for a year without success, I day dreamed of my name someday showing up on those leaderboards. More often than not, though, the leaderboards were showing the same names month to month. It's like out of hundreds of thousands of affiliate marketers, there were a dozen affiliates who knew something the rest of us bums did not.

If there's anything I learned about internet marketing, it's that success is rarely a result of raw talent or dumb luck. There's always a method, a strategy, modus operandi. And there's always someone who has already figured it out. The shortest path to success is modeling what the successful people do. Every name on those leaderboards represented someone who figured it out. All I had to do was reverse engineer what they were doing. So I did. I funnel hacked them. It's a term coined by Russell Brunson, the co-founder of Click Funnels. It's the process of studying your competitors' sales and marketing materials to analyze why it works and then applying the same techniques to your own marketing to improve results.

I funnel hacked the hell out of every website, email, offer, blog or membership site these super-affiliates had. If they released products – I bought them. If they publisher articles, I read them. If they ran ads, I clicked on them. If they publisher banners on their websites, I saved them. If they offered coaching, I played prospect. I wanted to know what their traffic sources were. I wanted to know everything about how they were generating leads.

What I found confused me. There was no one traffic source they all used. Some swore by banner ads. Others preached Google AdWords. Yet others were SEO (search engine optimization) experts. This was beyond frustrating. I still had no idea what to do to drive and convert leads. I tried all the methods these methods before. None of them worked for me. Either they were hiding their secrets well or I was missing something.

Turns out I was. The secret to their success was staring me in the face. I just didn't know what to look for. It was so obvious I couldn't believe it took me so long to realize it.

One night, I was switching between a YouTube motivational video and my Gmail inbox. I always did that when I was feeling overwhelmed. Around 9pm local time (roughly 2pm EST) my inbox exploded with emails from all the usual suspects. Within minutes I received 15 emails promoting the same affiliate program. 7 of those had the same subject line. That's when I had a blinding flash of insight.

They all had a large responsive email list of people who liked them and trusted them. It almost didn't matter how they built their email list. What mattered was they built one and were adding new email subscribers to their list every day. It gave them the ability to send a rush of targeted prospects with the desire and ability to buy to their affiliate link on launch day. This put them high on those leaderboards within hours.

What separated super-affiliates from loser-affiliates was their ability to send targeted traffic *on demand* to any affiliate offer they wish. Funny enough, the state of the industry didn't change since I discovered this concept.

You'd still be hard-pressed to find a super-affiliate who isn't building her email list. Sometimes, affiliate program owners won't allow you to promote their product unless you've got a large email list and you can prove it.

Here's why list building is the key to affiliate marketing success. Imagine you're driving traffic to your affiliate link at fifty cents per click. Don't get stuck on the number. Just follow the math. You run a 300-click campaign. It sets you back $150 in ad spend. You now need to make at least $150 in profit (probably double that in sales) just to break even. With an average click-to-sale conversion rate of 0.5% selling a $50 item, you're looking at roughly $50-$100 in sales. Even if you double your conversions, you only make $150 in sales. Still not enough to cover your ad spend considering fulfillment cost. And that's best case scenario. Realistic scenario is you make no sales, because the target market doesn't trust you yet and they need more time to make a decision.

Now let's run the same numbers, only this time we're going to build an email list. We'll run the same 300-click campaign to an email capture. This page is going to "squeeze" the visitor's email address. We'll probably get 130-150 visitors to share their email address to unlock the offer. Out of those 130-150 people, we'll get the same 0.5%-1% click-to-sale conversion resulting in anywhere from $50 to $150 in sales. We still haven't covered the cost of the entire ad campaign. But here's where the game changing difference really shows up. We now have an email list of 130-150 people we will follow up with. Over the course of the next 30-90 days we will close another 10%-30% of these people making anywhere from $650 to

$1950 in sales. At the very least, we'll generate a $500 profit from this campaign. And if our math is only half-right, and we get half the results, then we'll *only* profit $250-$325 on this campaign.

Here's where it gets really exciting. I didn't factor in any upsell commissions or long-term email list profits. The thing I learned about list building is while it takes time for people to decide to buy from you the first time, it gets easier the next time around. Overtime, list building gets easier, because your database of raving fans grows and with it, grows your profits. Price resistance and buyer resistance melt like butter.

As of writing this book, roughly a month ago, I've built a prelaunch email list of people interested in email marketing. It wasn't a huge list or anything. It was less than 1300 people; 1296 to be exact. I invited people to sign up on this email list if they were interested in working with me personally within the walls of a new coaching mastermind I started called List Building Lifestyle Club (visit www.listbuildinglifestyle.com for details).

About a week after making the announcement, I opened the doors to my mastermind. I sent out an email notifying these 1296 people the doors were open for 48 hours. We had nearly 300 people sign up at $97 a month. Nearly 30% took the annual upgrade at $697. 10% picked up the $1,000 upgrade. This one email promotion made me nearly $100,000 in 4 days. That's the power of an email list.

The money isn't the best part. It's the freedom. Whether you own a 1,000-person email list or a 10,000-person list, it takes just as much time and effort to run a promotion. Between 2015 and 2018 I've tripled my income. I went from making $600,000 and change a year to $1,800,000 and change annually. I didn't find work 3 times harder. I didn't find a way to squeeze 3X more hours in a day (although I wish I could). I didn't inject stem cell cocktail to have 3 times more energy. In fact, my routine didn't change much. What changed? My list tripled in size. I was promoting the same products and services. It's just I was showing up in front of 3 times more people.

You know the cliché posts internet marketers share on social media saying things like it's only 11:32am and I've already made $200? Or how they brag about coming back from a day trip to a lake and having made $2,000? It's their email list. List building is the key to passive income, because every part of it can be easily automated. In fact, these days, anytime a new subscriber joins my email list, they enroll in a 12-months email sequence designed to turn them into long term customers. Of course, I didn't start out with an exquisite email sequence. At first, I set up a very simplistic 7-day sequence. That was enough to get a trickle of sales. I grew from there. Email marketing is very forgiving. Even if you get it somewhat right, you'll still make way more money than most internet marketers.

The moment you see your own email list for what it truly is – a push-button traffic source you own – you're able to see and understand the true purpose of getting traffic to your website. It is not to make sales. It is to build your list.

By putting an opt in form in front of your visitors, you're turning a bunch of one-time clicks into repeat visitors you can send to your website whenever you feel like it. This simple switch to your traffic generation strategy immediately increases your conversions (because it takes multiple exposures to convert a new customer). Very quickly you become an owner of your own targeted traffic source that wants to do business with you. It makes growing a profitable online business so much easier.

Perry Marshall, the author of *80/20 Sales and Marketing* says, "There are all kinds of media and channels, but email is still the center of the marketing universe. It's permission to be inside your customer's personal space." Imagine what happens when you show up in your customers' personal space every day? They learn to like you, trust you and to not discard you as just another person who tries to sell them something. Because they made a decision to let you into their personal space by sharing their email address with you. There's a lot of power in that.

I'm not saying every person who subscribes to your email list will read every email you send out. It won't happen even if you're the Charles Dickens of email. It is likely that some people will read everything you mail. Most people will glance at every 7th or 15th email you send out. And that's a good thing. Eventually, when the stars align, they'll buy something. Just the other day I got an email from a subscriber saying, "Igor, I've been on your email list for 8 months. This last email you sent out finally got me. I'm in!" She proceeded to sign up for a $787 service and then upgraded to a $2,997 platinum offer the next day.

Some people, when they learn about list building, confuse having an email list with having social media followers. It is like saying Monopoly money and real money are the same thing, because they are printed on paper and kind of look the same. Try buying groceries with monopoly money and see what happens. You'll quickly learn the difference. 1 email subscriber does not equal 1 social media follower. It's not the same relationship. It's not the same buyer potential. It's not the same context.

There was a study conducted few years ago looking into the difference between people who check their email first thing in the morning and the people who check their Facebook first thing in the morning with relation to how these two groups of people patronize businesses and make buying decisions. The study uncovered a fascinating fact. People who check their email first thing in the morning tended to support businesses by buying their products. People, who check their social media first thing in the morning, felt they were supporting their favorite brands by liking their posts on social media. Now let's put it in the real world context. Imagine you operate a shoe store. Which customer would you prefer? The one who comes in once a day, tells you how much she likes your shoes and leaves without buying anything? Or would you rather serve someone who visits the store less frequently, but with intention to buy shoes and they feel good about their purchase? The latter sort of customer is not only more profitable to your business, but also more enjoyable to deal with.

Perhaps the biggest misconception internet marketers have about social media is the underlying cause of the prospects' behavior. People go on social media to escape the overwhelm of the day to day life. They escape hard decisions. They indulge in a mindless activity in the same way a person with an eating disorder gulps a bucket of Ben & Jerry when life gets a little too intense. An email subscriber is engaging you in a different way. They're seeking a solution. They're armed with intent to make a buyer decision. You don't need a PhD in sales psychology to see and understand why email traffic is superior to social media (and quite frankly to most other traffic sources).

From the moment I discovered all super-affiliates relied on their huge email lists to dominate leaderboards, I decided to not waste time. I set out to build a large responsive email list of my own. At first, I didn't even care if it was a quality list. I just wanted to build one, because I knew it's better to have an email list than not to have one.

I remember when I hit 2,200 subscribers. I knew my list wasn't of the highest quality. But I emailed it anyway. I emailed daily like it was some kind of religious ritual. For the most part, I didn't make anything. But I was already seeing trickles of sales here and there.

One day I jumped on a new product launch by Dan Brock called *Deadbeat Super Affiliate*. It was a $77 offer and it pad 75% commission funnel-wide. The day it was scheduled to launch I had to take my dad's friend to an airport. I came back home exhausted. My back hurt from driving our 98' Daewoo. I've had a lower back issue all my life. That day it flared up like a California wildfire. I would usually write emails about whatever was going on in my life at the time. That day was no exception. I told my email subscribers how much my back hurt and how it was probably because of all the time I'm spending behind the computer trying to figure out internet marketing every day. Then I segued into selling the product saying don't be like me. Here's a shortcut you can use, so you don't have to spend all these hours behind your computer trying to figure out how to make money online.

The email went out around 9pm. By midnight I made 17 sales.

I was blown away. I decided to carry on with the same message. For the next 7 days I emailed my list encouraging them to buy Dan's product, talking about my health issues, how time consuming internet marketing has become for me, how I wish I spent more time with my fiancé and anything revolving around my personal unfulfilled dreams. I finished the affiliate competition 13th out of 20.

I was on the leaderboard, baby! I was finally a super-affiliate!

Even if accidental, this success proved I was right to build an email list. And even though the vast majority of my subscribers chose not to buy from me right away, I now knew it didn't matter. Because eventually, if they see the right offer presented to them at the right angle at the right time – they will buy.

It's been years since I've tapped into this secret. Things almost didn't change. I still email my list every day. I still share my personal life with my subscribers when I get a chance. Nowadays, however, I dominate affiliate promotions with ease. An average affiliate promotion I participate in usually brings in somewhere between $20,000 and $70,000 in commissions. I don't share this to brag, but help you see and understand email marketing is not dead. In fact, email is the easiest way to a six-figure income from scratch online. Allow me to show you how in the next chapter.

Would you like to get access to my most profitable affiliate email campaigns? Visit www.igor.cx/tools for details

Chapter 5
Rapid Automated Traffic

Imagine you're an aspiring female fitness guru. You would like to help women over 40 lose weight quickly with a non-intrusive low-will-power-required diet specifically designed for the female body. In the last year you helped 5 women lose 10 lbs. in 10 days. You documented these case studies. Now you're ready to market your product.

The dinosaur approach is to run cold ads in yellow pages, in the local paper and to hand out fliers in the Walmart parking lot. If you're ambitious, you could run radio ads on your local station or conduct free seminars in Holiday Inn lobby.

The advanced approach is to run cold ads in media your ideal customers subscribe to such as Women's Health, Runners World, Shape, Experience Life, Pilates Style, etc. This would require a huge budget, of course, but it won't be as expensive as running an ad on national TV. This would also require you to hire an ad writing specialist (aka copywriter) who knows what they're doing, because they'll be running ads with your money. Oh, and you'll also need a website or a hotline your potential customers can call, in order to submit their order. And someone will have to pick up the phone around the clock, so you'll probably need to hire someone to do that or give up personal life for a while and do it yourself.

If you're not into print media, you can try social media. Join a bunch of fitness groups for women and blast your website all over the place. Hopefully, before you're kicked out of the group, you'll generate some interest. Maybe you can build a fan page and have all your friends "like" it. Chances of you going viral are, of course, slimmer than slim. But hey, at least it's free, right?

Okay, let's get serious. There's no such thing as free, remember? Let's do the right thing and run Facebook ads. Let's hire a videographer to create a series of promotional videos with ambiguous imagery announcing an amazing new diet for women over 40 that's working like gangbusters. And to keep the risks down to a minimum, let's set out daily ad budget to $10 a day. Ideally, we'll scale this campaign to $1,000 a day within a few months, because Facebook allows us to target women over 40, which would naturally lead us believe it's a perfect match.

In an ideal world, we would be rich. Here is what happens in the real world.

First, you'll pay out the nose to a video crew to create your ads. These ads won't turn out nowhere near what you expected, but you will reluctantly use them, because you won't be able to afford a remake. Then, you'll get lost in the ad targeting options. Since you're working with a limited budget, you wouldn't be able to test every single one of the two dozen placement and targeting options you need to choose from. In your attempt to figure it out, you'll binge Facebook ads tutorials on YouTube and buy 2 courses promising to reveal the secrets to guaranteed targeting success. Unless you've already given up like most people, you'll then spend a good 2 weeks trying to figure out tracking pixels, sub IDs, security certificates and php callbacks. See where I'm going with this? We still haven't even started talking about legal disclaimers or landing pages or sales copy or offer optimization or even retargeting.

But let's say you're a special kind of marketer and you figured it all out. You're running ads. Your ads are converting. Against all odds, you're making money. Sometime within the next 30 days you will make up and won't see any clicks, leads or sales in your account. It will feel like someone just turned off your entire business. What happened? While you were peacefully dreaming of buying the Bentley you've always wanted, some pimple-faced geek in the Facebook headquarters who has no understanding of your business, decided to disable your ad account for policy violation. Just like that.

This isn't a made up scenario. Although I changed a few details, that's exactly what happened to me. I had a program helping people build traffic businesses. I was spending $2,000 a day on Facebook ads. One day my account showed a policy violation notice. I emailed them. I submitted support tickets. I consulted Facebook ads experts. No use. They turned me off. Just like that, a $100,000 a month income stream gone with a push of a button.

I've made several attempts to get back on Facebook. All ended in the exact same way. Whether it was 6 days or 6 weeks or even 6 months, eventually Facebook shut me down. It didn't matter what I was spending or what I was promoting or how I was promoting it. The end result was always the same.

At first it didn't make sense to me. If Facebook's primary source of income was advertising, why ban advertisers? Especially the ones who spend a lot of money every day? Facebook's mission is to create ultimate user experience and increase engagement. It's not to help their advertisers make more sales (that would lead to them spending more money). In fact, Facebook recently announced their newsfeed has become so crowded with ads they've decided to double advertising tariffs. A friend internet marketer who used to generate leads almost exclusively through Facebook ads up until that announcement said their customer acquisition cost skyrocketed from $250-$400 per sale to $800-$1200 per sale as a result. They dropped Facebook ads within a few months. Another friend who runs a multi-million-dollar online business said he's spending $125,000 per month on Facebook ads and he's happy if he's making 20% of his investment back at this point.

If you're a billion-dollar conglomerate like Coca-Cola or Apple looking to do a brand exposure campaign, Facebook is a great way to do that. But if you're a start-up looking to self-fund your growth, pay per click ad networks are unlikely to help you scale. You need a low-tech traffic generation strategy that puts you in front of warm leads. Preferably, leads who have expressed interest in the products and services you're marketing. This traffic source needs to be scalable on demand. It needs to be cost-effective. Ideally, it should be a lead source you won't get "slapped" out of or banned from. It should be just as easy, fast and cost effective today as it will be a year from now or 5 years from now. Traffic source you can build on knowing the carpet won't be pulled from underneath your feet when you least expect it.

Jeff Bezos, CEO of Amazon once said he gets asked a lot about what's going to change in the next 10 years. He said it's his least favorite question, because you can't build long-term success on something that's going to change. Strong foundations are built on things that don't change.

Ask yourself what's not going to change in the next 10 years? Email. Just like email didn't kill the phone, Kindle didn't kill physical books, social media didn't kill email. Email is still one of 3 primary communication tools we use. We need an email address to get our cell phone bill, we sign contracts over email, we book appointments with email, we get our Amazon receipts via email, we even need an email address to create a Facebook account.

Earlier I shared how email marketing changed my life. It became the tool I used to convert cold visitors into buyers. I was making money, but I was still struggling to create a stable and affordable flow of new customers. Most traffic campaigns bombed. The one that worked were hard to replicate and scale. My successes weren't consistent. Every campaign seemed scarier than the last.

One day I stumbled into a community of list builders who did something I never considered. They promoted each other's offers to their email lists. This strategy would later become known as ad swapping. At the time, it was still a bizarre concept, because internet marketers tended to be overprotective of their email lists. To me, it made perfect sense. Instead of promoting affiliate offers every day of the week, why not take two days to swap other list builders and grow your email list for free?

There was one problem though. My list was only couple of thousand people. You needed at least 10,000 email subscribers to qualify for an ad swap. After getting a few rejections, I had an idea. I approached several medium sized list owners with a paid promo proposal. It would work exactly like an ad swap would, only instead of emailing my list with their offer, I would just pay them a fee upfront based on the approximate number of unique visitors they sent me.

It worked. It worked so well, in fact, I nearly broke even on the first run. I walked away with a few hundred new opt ins on my email list *and* enough revenue to call it a success. I continued running these campaigns with a handful of other list builders on a monthly basis until I reached 20,000 email subscribers on my list. At that point, in addition to running these solo email ad campaigns I swapped several times a week. The more my list grew, the more grew my income. Within 6 months I scaled from $500 a month to $10,000 a month using this one strategy. The rest is history.

This worked so much better than running cold ads, because I was putting my offer in front of people who have already expressed an interest in similar products. Some of them have micro-committed in a form of giving up their private information (their email address) in exchange for relevant information. Others have gone as far as buying a product. More, I was being endorsed by someone they trusted – the email list owner. It made a huge difference in conversions.

Believe it or not, it gets better. Since there was no ad network that would create a global bidding platform, the price per click these email list owners were charging was a fraction of the going industry rates on Google AdWords. I wasn't only getting higher conversions, because I didn't have to waste time and money qualifying leads. It was also costing me less to drive traffic and I needed to make less on the back end to recoup my investment. It went a long way towards helping me bootstrap my business to six-figures that year.

Did things change since then? Yes, they did. Now it's much easier to get email solo ads (aka email endorsement traffic) for virtually any product or niche. At the time, I was limited to an intimate group of open-minded list builders. These days, however, you can get in front of hundreds of thousands of email subscribers on any topic from weight loss to crypto.

You're probably thinking, "Igor, why would they allow me to do that? Why would they allow me to tap their email list for a fee?" Think about it. Isn't that exactly what every single influencer in the history of media had done to leverage their position?

Oprah endorsed Obama during both of his successful presidential runs. You'd be naïve to think she'd gone through all the trouble of flying around the country co-hosting rallies with him, just because she believed in the cause. She probably got compensated somehow. Why did Obama pick Oprah? Because of her reach. She's been the queen of talk show TV for years. She probably has more influence over people's opinions than anyone in the United States. Brilliant move on Obama's part.

"Igor, that's a bit of an extreme example because I'm not a celebrity and I'm not running for president." Fine. What about book promotions? You've probably seen lots of cross promotions between authors. What about Facebook? Facebook built an audience for a few years and then, the first thing they've done to monetize the audience would allow people to run ads to that audience. Google has become the richest company in the world by building an audience and selling ads to that audience.

Email is just another form of media. Running an email campaign to a list is same as broadcasting an ad to radio listeners. Same way radio and TV stations sell ads to make money, email marketers do too.

This traffic strategy is accessible. There's no barrier to entry. You can just as easily secure a $50 solo ad to a small email list (or a small portion of a big email list) as you can drop $5,000 on a massive email drop to hundreds of thousands of email subscribers. I recommend starting slow. Once you've found email lists that convert for you (not all will convert equally well), scale those. Rinse and repeat until you're tapping several email lists on monthly basis for a stable flow of leads.

You can now see and understand how to generate targeted traffic on demand at a highly-affordable price. All you need to do is conduct some research in your niche and find out who's building an email list you can run a solo ad to. Subscribe to these email lists. Get a feel for what they are emailing. Note how often they email. You'll probably notice they email their subscribers once a month or once or twice a week at most. Why is it important? Because agreeing to mail your solo ad they won't be hurting their business. It won't break their rigid schedule or otherwise interfere with anything they got going on. It's just an easy extra income for them and an easy way to build your email list for you.

Find out the best places to buy email solo ads visit www.igor.cx/tools

Chapter 6
How To Find Email Lists That Convert Without Breaking The Bank

Amid the flagship fashion stores of the world's most luxurious shopping center in the Ginza district of Chuo, Tokyo stands old grey office building. In its basement sits Sukiyabashi Jiro, a 10-seat sushi bar. It has no waiting area, reservation desk, parking lot or even a bathroom on the premises. But it is the only sushi bar in the world to have earned 3 Michelin stars. The owner named Jiro Ono is an 86-year old sushi Michelangelo. He's widely recognized as the world's #1 sushi chef. Jiro's restaurant has a 3-year waiting list and you're allowed to stay for no longer than 15 minutes.

Jiro's older son Yoshikazu has been 2nd in command for a very long time. He's waiting to take the reins of the family legacy when Jiro steps down. Until then, he's in charge of the ingredients. Every morning he makes his way to a local fish market where, just like Jiro has been for the last 40 years, he's greeted by a fish supplier. The supplier is already prepping Yoshikazu's order. Jiro's first born been taught by his father, the sushi master, how the ingredients play a critical role in making world class sushi. That's why they stuck with the same supplier for decades. Yoshikazu knows working with the wrong ingredients can ruin not only customers' meal, but Jiro's impeccable reputation.

Choosing an email list to work with is what choosing ingredients is to making sushi. If you run a great offer to a bad email list, you will not convert. And sometimes, you'll run a bad offer to a quality list and you'll come on top. List's data quality makes all the difference in the world.

How can you know which email lists are quality and which aren't? Run small tests before you scale. The mistake I see many people make is hoping to hit a homerun the first time the run a solo ad. But that's kind of like marrying the first person you date. It's possible. But unlikely. By testing a segment, you can put a little bit of money at risk to find out whether the email list you're working with is right for you. If it is, then you can buy a solo ad to a larger segment. If not, you move on to testing the next list.

For example, let's say you negotiated an email solo ad with a 100,000 subscriber email list for $1,000. You could run an ad to the entire list, if you're fine with risking a thousand dollars. If you're risk-averse, like me, you'd want to propose a $100 promotion to a segment of 10,000 subscribers as a test and scale if you get results. This strategy allows you to get better mileage from your advertising dollars by testing several sources at the same time.

Throttling your solo ads allows protects you against scams. Remember, there's no governing email marketing body overseeing the solo ad industry. There's no traffic police. It's a wild-wild west out there. On one hand, it allows you and me to get traffic knowing we won't get slapped. On the other hand, it creates a large space for charlatans and double-dealers to sell fake traffic.

Several years ago I was speaking at an email marketing conference in Orlando. There I met an internet marketer who said he had a lot of traffic. He knew I was buying. He offered me a deal too good to pass up. We shook on it. When I came back home, I set up a new campaign with him. I didn't throttle my ad spend. I didn't check my stats. I just trusted him because I met him in person and he seemed trustworthy to me.

The damages caught up with me few months later. Reviewing weekly stats, I noticed an unusually bad campaign. At the time I was already making good money, so it was unusual for me to see no return when I ran traffic. Typical campaign would still produce 25%-30% return on the low end. This campaign, however, was showing 100% loss. I pulled up last month's reports and saw the same pattern. Something wasn't right.

Upon further investigation I tracked the traffic back to the "trustworthy" buddy from the conference. We were getting 10,000 clicks a week from him. All dead. The email subscribers we generated from his traffic never opened our emails. An unusually high percentage of those subscribers "bounced." It means they were full inboxes, fake inboxes or used-to-be-real inboxes that since turned into spam-traps. Either way, it wasn't looking good. I was paying for duds.

Before I would confront him, I conducted one last check. We use tracking software called HotJar (www.hotjar.com) to better understand user behavior. This software records visitor behavior, tracks cursor activity, visual heat maps and a bunch of other cool stuff. It also tracks device, screen resolution, IP address, operating system and anything else you could wish for.

I pulled a few IP addresses from my email autoresponder and ran them through our HotJar database. I discovered the screen dimensions of the traffic this person was sending me were 100x2. If you're not familiar with screen dimension standards, all you need to know is screens like that don't exist. Using a screen like that to browse the internet would be like watching a rock concert through half a peep hole.

I took this proof to him and demanded my money back. He refunded me the same day knowing how much influence I command in the industry. Few weeks later he disappeared completely. I was lucky to get my money back because I was experienced. But think of all the people he scammed who didn't even know what he'd done to them.

Unfortunately, it's just one of several ways to get conned when buying email traffic. You can be working with a reseller who resells your traffic at a markup to someone else. They could be charging you a dollar a click and then reselling your order to someone else at 30 cents a click. I know people who make a living this way. Not all resellers are bad though. There are traffic brokers who can get you specific sources you can't otherwise access on your own.

Another thing to look out for is lead injection. Skilled hackers know how to "backdoor" leads into your system. Leads that had no intention to getting on your email list in the first place. When they start getting emails from you they hit the spam button. This could quickly cost you're your email autoresponder account.

You also want to make sure you're getting top-tier traffic when you buy solo ads. I purchased an email drop from an affiliate marketing authority site. They sent a lot of traffic, but over 50% was from places like Eastern Europe, India and Africa. As someone who was born in Ukraine and lived in the Middle East for 18 years, I know to not expect much from this traffic. Not because Eastern Europeans, Africans and Hindu folk are bad people. It's just they are victims of the economy. For example, many of them don't speak English well. They struggle to understand what I'm selling. Even if they want what I'm selling, many times they can't buy it because these countries offer limited credit options. They couldn't buy my products even if they wanted. Another thing is the exchange rate. For an American or a Canadian $97 isn't a huge investment. For some citizens of India, it's their entire monthly wage.

Another thing to look out for would be beaten-to-death email lists. There are people out there who figured out they can sell traffic for a living. I'm one of them. I won't hide it. I run and operate Igor Solo Ads, world's largest solo ad agency (www.IgorSoloAds.com). Helping people build their own profitable email list is my business. One of the ways I do that is by driving traffic for them from my email list.

The difference between someone like me and a run-of-the-mill solo ad seller is I generate 4,000-12,000 new email leads a day. I keep my email list fresh. Many solo ad sellers can't afford to invest as much as I do in lead generation. They just sell clicks and hammer their email list to squeeze every last bit of blood out of it until it becomes unresponsive. These people sell email traffic at an unusually low rate. Typically, under ¢50 per click. Their philosophy is it's better to sell 100 clicks and make a guaranteed $50 then promote an offer and make nothing. Don't waste your money with these scoundrels.

Finally, one last warning, be wary of solo ad directories. These are traffic marketplaces that connected buyers and sellers in the same way Uber connects people looking for a ride with drivers willing to chauffer people for a fee. When you sign up, you are being presented with a list of traffic guns for hire. There's not much differentiating them aside from their list size, price per click and reviews. Most people go with solo ad sellers with highest rating. That's a mistake, because most of these ratings aren't real. I learned about it by accident.

Back in the day, I was a member of an ad swap website where people with email lists could swap promotions. Remember, an email ad swap is same as an email solo ad but instead of paying for traffic, you barter solo ads. One time I was swapping with another internet marketer. On my end, things were looking great. I was getting opt ins and sales. For him, it didn't go as well. In fact, he contacted me a few hours after we started asking to stop the traffic, because he was getting bad results. He said he didn't know what kind of traffic I sending him, but he wanted nothing to do with it. He was very upset with me. To this day, I don't know what happened, but what stands out in my memory is what he said next. He said he didn't want any bad blood, so he will rate me as a 5-star ad swap partner and he expects me to do the same. In spite of getting terrible results with my traffic, he rated me as one of the best swap partners he had. I didn't argue. We exchanged 5-star ratings and never worked together again. That was the last time I used that site to swap another marketer. It shattered my trust in the rating system which was pretty much the only way to tell who you're dealing with.

Okay, Igor, but what do ad swaps have to do with solo ad marketplaces? Well, the site I'm talking about has since then been rebranded and is now the largest solo ad marketplace. The name, logo and interface are all different. But it's the same faulty rating system. You have to sift through lots of dirt to find decent traffic there. Why? Because nobody's posting negative reviews on the site. If a buyer isn't satisfied, more often than not, the seller offers a full refund or additional traffic to keep the buyer happy. Besides, the website owner gets a cut of every transaction on the site. They're financially interested in rating-driven system, because it puts more money in their pocket.

Advertising to the right email list is half the battle. The other half is converting the leads. Next chapter breaks down the 80/20 of turning email leads into long-term profits.

Access free training showing how to vet email traffic providers with 7 simple questions at www.igor.cx/tools

Chapter 7
Massive Passive Email Income

So here I was, running traffic, building my email list and making some of my money back in the process. For every 100 new subscribers I was generating on my email list I was averaging 2 paying customers. That was enough to recoup a portion of the investment, but not all of it. After a few months of running traffic, I had tens of thousands of non-paying email subscribers and a handful of customers.

At first I thought my sales copy wasn't good enough. I hired a copywriting coach who helped me rewrite my sales page. We saw a 0.3% sales bump. Enough to put a smile on my face. Not enough to recoup my traffic investment in full. I repositioned the offer. I extended my guarantee. I collected more case studies. I followed every direct response textbook to a "t." I checked off every box of every "conversion" checklist if one existed. It seemed like nothing I did moved the needle.

They say a problem well defined is half solved. I decided to redefine my challenge. Instead of trying to pull more sales on the front end, I shifted my focus to the 98% of my list that chose not to buy from me. I've had thousands of potential sales just waiting to happen. I just had to figure out how to turn these free email addresses into paying customers.

I knew it was a matter of saying the right thing. I just didn't know what to say or how to say it. I wasn't a great writer. English wasn't even my native language. I was born in Ukraine, so my native language was Russian. My 2nd language was Hebrew because I lived in Israel for 18 years. I learned English by watching TV shows with subtitles and instant messaging with friends from a gaming community I was a part of in my teens. Still, I wrote English better than I spoke it. And I had a spell checker and a thesaurus to assist me. I'm not saying I wasn't scared. Email marketing, and specifically email writing, frightened me out of my wits. It's just the eventuality of running out of money scared me even more.

Before I could start writing, I needed to know what to write about. I've had no idea what these people wanted. I didn't know how to approach them. Do I just pitch them? Or do I email 80% content and pitch only 20% of the time. I couldn't get a straight answer. Email marketing advice I came across in my research was contradicting. Some people said I should email my list once a month. Others suggested weekly emails. Some said to never pitch in my emails. Others suggested to pitch sometimes, but to never make dry offers. Some gurus claimed to have developed the perfect content-pitch ratio and that supposedly if you stuck to this ratio, you'd always make sales with your email list. I followed their suggested structure. Unfortunately, none of these approaches turned out effective. I wasted 6 months putting each method to the test with my email list. In the process I must've pissed off half my list, because that's how many people I lost to unsubscribes and spam complaints.

Losing half my list didn't bother me as much as the fact I was attempting random tactics without logic or reasoning. I like to know the "why" behind the "how." I would turn in my bed at night with all these questions running through my mind. Are my email subscribers even interested in buying from me? If they are, why are they not buying? What are they expecting me to say? What am I not saying to help them see and understand they should work with me? Are they even getting my emails? What do they want? What's the difference between my emails (that don't work) and someone else's emails that produce tons of sales?

There's an old adage in online marketing saying people buy from people who they like and trust. It's not quite accurate. Most people trying to market products online are nice likeable people. It doesn't make them great marketers. In fact, more often than not, their income is oppositely-proportionate to how nice they are.

One of the most common pieces of advice floating around the internet is to "get yourself out there." It states you should open up your personal life to your customers to make them like you. Apparently, if they know you're a dog person and what your mother's boyfriend's sister's middle name is, it practically guarantees a sale. No, it does not. People don't care about you.

Your potential customers are concerned with one thing – themselves. Their minds are tuned to one radio station – WIIFM (What's In It For Me?). Don't believe me? Next time you meet someone, don't talk about anything other than your problems. Notice how quickly this person, no matter how nice, "checks out" of the conversation. Alternatively, you could also try to talk about nothing but *their* problems by asking questions about their life, their challenges, things that concern them and their most annoying problems. Notice how quickly they open up to you. They can't help it. It's human nature.

Your email subscribers don't care what you're marketing and how much it costs, until they know you understand what they're going through right now. It's no longer enough to just to offer a solution to problem. Solutions are dime a dozen. So are experts. So what if you're world's foremost authority on shredded cheese? Thing is, people get pitched so many times throughout the day, they've learned to tune out anything even remotely resembling a sales pitch. That is, until they believe you understand them.

If you can show your target market you get where they're coming from by talking to them about their problems, fears, desires and suspicions, they will flock to you for a solution. You won't need to push it on them or look for ways to disguise your sales pitch with content. They will be asking you to do it. When someone helps us understand our problems, we hope this person can offer us a solution. When they do – we take it with almost no resistance. And this changes the whole dynamic of the marketing dialogue, because now it's no longer you pushing your product with an agenda. It's them asking for a solution to their problem from someone they trust.

Besides not having to hard-close anyone, you'll also never run out of things to talk about in your emails, as long as you remember people think about their own problems all day every day. You can never be boring to a woman with a weight loss problem by talking about how hard it is to lose pregnancy fat. You can never be boring to a mechanic talking about the BMW 7-Series they've been working on in their spare time for the last 16 years. You can never be boring to a millionaire talking about new tax legislation.

How often should you email your list? Every. Single. Day. I know this makes you cringe. I know this makes you feel like a spammer. And you should do it anyway.

Common email wisdom says you should follow up with your email subscribers for about 14 days before writing them off as non-responsive or not interested. It stems from another common belief stating that an average of 7 exposures to an offer is required to close a sale. I followed this strategy with the first email list I ever built for a network marketing opportunity. I generated over 1,000 subscribers on that email list and I recruited no one into my downline. What did I do with all these subscribers after 14 days? Nothing. They were just sitting there. I emailed them once 8 months later. I've had 3 opens, 1 click and 1 spam complaint. My subscribers have forgotten about me. The window of opportunity was lost.

Email marketing isn't a sprint. It's a marathon. The vast majority of email opt ins on your email list are interested but they're not ready to buy yet. For some it's about personal circumstances while others may need to be educated before they'll feel comfortable making a buying decision. Whatever their excuse, it's normal for prospects delay buying decisions. We're being told to measure 7 times before we cut since we're kids. We're told stories educating us about avoiding being hasty with our decisions like the little red riding hood. It isn't a story about a little girl who wanted to do something nice for her grandma. It's a story about gullibility. It's a story about questioning stranger's intentions. It's a story about healthy skepticism. Is it any wonder even people who need our products and services most make it so hard for us to help them? Nope. Not at all.

You can have world's most amazing offer and they may know they need it more than anything right now – and yet – they'll find a reason why buying right now isn't right for them. Until one day, they'll get that one email from you that pushes them over the fence. The other day a client emailed me saying she's been on my email list for 8 months and how this one email about traffic finally "got her." It's almost like she was waiting for the right excuse to commit. Another client told me he was on my email list for years and that he finally decided to work with me because his job contract was expiring and he needed to get his online business going.

It doesn't matter what the reason they don't want to buy now is. What matters is – your emails will be there when they're ready, offering them a way to do it. Which bring us to the final question – how often should you pitch your product in your emails?

I was once talking to a coaching client who complained she had a list of 2,700 email subscribers. She said she was emailing her list every day, as instructed, but she wasn't making money. I asked her what she was mailing. She said she was mostly sending out useful articles and videos. She wanted her subscribers to like her. I asked how often was she pitching her product. She said she didn't. She said she was hoping her subscribers like her so much, they'd proactively seek out her product online.

Your email marketing income is directly proportionate to the amount of offers you make to your email subscribers. If you're building an email list to make money (and if not, you shouldn't be building a list in the first place), you should pitch your offer in every email. The resistance to making frequent offers comes from the conditioning people have of either being bad at sales or feeling bad about selling, because it's unethical.

I used to feel this way about selling because I was raised by a music teacher who never made much money in her life and who never considered money to be important. If you're armed with the same belief, consider the following scenario. You founded a cancer-treating machine. This machine is capable of healing cancer for 7 out of 10 patients. Your neighbor, John, has a 12-year-old daughter Jessica. Jessica has been diagnosed with stage 2 cancer. The treatment costs $14,000. You know John doesn't have this kind of money saved up. But he could get it, if he was willing to borrow it or if he was willing to sell his truck and jet ski. What would you do? Would you casually mention it to John over coffee once? Or would you nag John every single day, knocking on his door, calling him, sending him mail pigeons and doing whatever necessary to get his attention to give him an opportunity to save his daughter's life? It would be your moral and ethical obligation to "sell" John on your machine. It would be the *right thing to do.*

If you don't feel comfortable pitching your product every day (even though your email subscribers opted in to learn more about it indicating their interest), consider getting something else to market, because chances are you don't believe in your product.

You now know 3 big secrets to email marketing success. You know what to talk about in your email to always be interesting and relevant to your email subscribers. You know you need to email your list every day, because email marketing is a marathon and not a sprint. You know it's your ethical responsibility to pitch in every email, because if you don't, you're depriving your clients of the opportunity to solve their problems. Logically, all this could be making perfect sense to you, but you may still find yourself resisting emailing your list. Many people try to hit a homerun the first time they step up to the plate. They put so much pressure on themselves to write the perfect email, they fail before they start. Most never send out the first email.

If you writing emails sounds scary, just remember, email marketing is forgiving. Rather than looking for the homerun, treat each email as a training swing. Eventually, just like a river made of dozens of streams, you'll develop lots of "sales streams" which would together create big passive income. And if your next email bombs, just take note of what you shouldn't say next time and try again tomorrow.

Driving traffic without an email follow up sequence is a lot like pouring water in a leaking bucket. Writing emails is scary, if you never done it before. If you'd like Igor to write your follow up email sequence for you visit www.igor.cx/tools for details

Chapter 8
How To Find Products That Sell

The conventional approach to starting a new business is creating or sourcing a product first and looking for ways to sell it second. That's most certainty the approach I took with my business when I started. The biggest question on my mind wasn't how to get traffic, but rather what should I be selling. It was a mistake.

The late Gary Halbert said the most profitable habit you can cultivate is to always be on the lookout for hungry markets. These are groups of people who have demonstrated they are starving (or at least showed interest in) for some particular type of product or service. To paraphrase the late direct marketing genius, you should first look for a hungry traffic source. Once you found one, offer the market what it wants.

Don't bother trying to disrupt the marketplace by investing $150,000 in a new tech start up. You can do it after you've made your first million. For now, focus on getting your business off the ground, by reaching for the lowest hanging fruit. In fact, nowadays, whenever I am starting a new business, I often create the product after I validate in the market by making several sales. If my test fails, I don't have to waste time and money on creating a failing product. If it works, it becomes a self-funded business from day one.

This is very unconventional approach unknown to traditional business thinkers. But it works. While Joe Blow rents out an office space, buys a desk and a chair, frames their MBA and stocks up on office supplies... I've already tested my idea, got proof of concept and generated enough paying customers to self-fund the project in the critical startup phase.

So how do you test your product idea quickly? What if you don't have any ideas to test? Where can you find products to promote quickly and without taking on any commitments or making huge investments? Should you create a product from scratch or should you source a product from China?

The first product I ever sold was a network marketing opportunity. My first internet marketing mentor suggested a I promote a $10/mo. MLM called Global Domains International where I earned a dollar per referral. If I referred three friends who each referred three friends... you know the drill. I never made it big in GDI, but it is through MLM I discovered a fascinating business model called affiliate marketing.

While struggling to make money with GDI, I spent a small fortune on home study courses, software, mentoring, plugins, themes, masterminds, and seminars. One day, I was considering buying a WordPress theme called *Thesis.*

It cost $297. I was searching for some Thesis reviews because I was on the fence when I stumbled into a blog post by an affiliate marketer who offered a $60 discount on Thesis theme if you bought it through his affiliate link.

It turned out he was getting $120 commission for each referral, so it made sense for him to kick back half of it to the customer (me and hundreds of people like me) and keep $60 than making nothing at all. I bought through his link. That transaction changed my life forever. I dropped out of MLM and pursued affiliate marketing instead. It was clearly the superior model for me.

First, I didn't have to get positioned or "qualify" to get paid. Most affiliate programs were free to join unlike network marketing opportunities all of whom require you to use the product in order to promote it. In fact, it's very common for MLMers to get a monthly lotion and potion shipment (that piles dust in their garage or gets thrown into the trash) just so they qualify to get paid.

Second, I wasn't pushing sprays, vitamins and magic powder on people. It became easier to talk to people, because I wasn't perceived as a pyramid scheme pusher anymore. Now, don't get me wrong. I love MLM. In fact, these days I work with some of the biggest network marketing teams in the world. It's just at the time, I just didn't have the marketing skills required to make it big in MLM.

Promoting network marketing opportunities required going through tons of rejection. Every "yes" was preceded by a hundred "no"s. It wasn't my idea of a great way to make a living. Affiliate marketing was way easier. I was no longer one of those guys who promotes pyramid schemes. I became a helpful advisor to people who were already looking for ways to solve specific problems. I wasn't trying to sell them something they didn't want. I tapped into an existing desire and gave people *exactly what they wanted!* Best part, these people were willing to invest in the solutions I was offering.

Third, the money was good, way better than MLM. The typical MLM pays 15%–35% commissions. Typical affiliate program pays 50%–75% commission. Some pay 100%. In addition, there were many affiliate programs offering recurring commissions for services people used on a monthly basis, like hosting and email autoresponders.

Fourth, unlike network marketing opportunities that required one-on-one closing, three-way calls, prospecting, group meetings, and a bunch of other things I sucked at, affiliate marketing offers came with a high-converting website that did all the selling for me. I didn't have to hire a graphic designer or a copywriter. I didn't have to create the content or code the software. My job was simple. I had to drive targeted clicks to my affiliate website and cash in.

Finally, unlike network marketing companies, many affiliate marketing programs paid out instantly to my PayPal account. The money was split immediately between the product creator and me. Getting my money fast was imperative to my success because I was putting all of it right back into traffic to build my email list. Of course, this discovery was accidental, but later I learned the importance of not having a barrier between me and the commissions I was earning.

A friend of mine runs an Airbnb business. He invested in several properties in St Petersburg, Russia just before the FIFA World Cup. He built a great profile, with high ratings and quickly sold out his properties 6 month in advance. One day he phoned me asking for a loan of $3,000 to pay off some bills. I asked him how could he behind on his bills with such a successful business. He said while his properties were booked months in advance and there was no shortage of new requests coming in, he wouldn't be getting the money until 90 days after the customers check out. He thought he could live off his savings, but quickly learned he was wrong.

There was just one downside to affiliate marketing. When I referred a sale, I didn't keep the buyer. I didn't know at the time that the key to long term success was to build a buyer list of my own. Michael Masterson in his book *Ready, Fire, Aim* calls it reaching a critical mass of good paying customers who patronize your business on an ongoing basis. This is important, if you'd like to scale your online business to $1,000,000 or more per year.

At the time, I wasn't trying to build the world's largest enterprise. I was just trying to fire my boss. For that, I needed $1,000 a week in net profit. It can be easily done promoting other people's products. In fact, just in the last 6 months my business generated over $500,000 in sales with affiliate promotions alone.

I recommend affiliate marketing for anyone who wants to build an online business but doesn't have a product, a service, a skill, or enough creativity to create their own products. It is a very easy way to get your new online business off the ground without unnecessary investments in product development, hiring copywriters or even building your own websites.

You can create a free ClickBank.com account right now and gain instant access to thousands of products to promote as an affiliate across dozens of niches, from making money online to dog grooming to makeup to supplements to losing weight to fixing your marriage. ClickBank is one of several digital marketplaces where average people can pick and choose products to promote and get paid generous commissions on referrals. You don't need a degree or fancy letters after your name. If you're 18 or older, you're qualified.

Digital marketplaces like ClickBank are a blessing for people like you and me because they take care of everything. They process the orders and facilitate product delivery. They connect product creators and affiliates without the need for the two to "work things out." There are no contracts for you to sign. You don't need to worry about customer support. You can even earn money as an affiliate without your customers even knowing your real name or address. In fact, there's a whole slew of people I call underground super-affiliates who make hundreds of thousands of dollars in commissions each month without their friends and family ever knowing it.

In fact, before you start following the blueprint I laid out for you in this book, I'm excited for you to find out exactly what your life may look like if you do as I suggest.

Next chapter introduces you to one of my students (who turned into one of my best friends) who started out, just like you, slaving 9 to 5 for minimum wage and who quickly rose to become one of the world's top super-affiliates using list building and solo ads.

Not sure what to promote? Get an up-to-date list of Igor's recommended high-converting offers at www.igor.cx/tools

Case Study: From Zero to $17,000 in 90 Days

Dear reader, my name is David Dekel and I am a full-time list builder. Few years ago I came across Igor and he changed my life. Igor asked me to share my story with you, to help you see and understand how quickly your life can change, if you follow the advice in the pages of this book. I don't know you, but trust me, wherever you are right now, I've been there. Whatever you think you've tried, and it hasn't worked, I've tried it, and it probably hasn't worked for me, either.

Before deciding to start my own online business, I was working for a very large established organization. I had a good job by a lot of people's standards. At the end of 2012, I wanted to take a Christmas vacation. I knocked on my boss's door and said, "Hey, Dan, I have some personal things going on at the end of December, and I wanted to take some time off."

It was my birthday. Also, my daughter turned one. It was Christmas. I wanted to take some time off and enjoy some family time with my daughter. Before I even got a chance to leave the office, he said, "No, because if I give you any time off, I'm going to have to give everybody else time off, too."

That sucked. I was the guy who showed up. I never missed a work day or took sick leave. I was a good employee by many people's standards. He also said, "Look, we have a big quota to meet before the end of the year." I figured, "Okay. You know what? Let me go ahead and put in the hours."

I kept my head down and worked hard. At the end of the month, we had met our quota. I got my check, and I looked at it. It was the same amount I made every other month down to the penny. I thought, "Man, I put in all this over time and that's what I get?" I worked my butt off. I put in 12-, 13-, 14-hour days that month! I thought there'd be a little something extra!

I called the head office and said, "Hey, I think there's something wrong with my check, because it is supposed to be bigger." They replied, "There's nothing wrong with it. You don't get paid by the hour. You get paid a global amount regardless of how many hours you put in."

It looks like no one bothered telling me that before I put in all those extra hours. That was a huge red flag for me. I realized I was a number on a spreadsheet. If you're working for a big company right now, trust me, as important as you are, you're probably a number, too.

You're a robot that comes in every day, produces a product, and leaves. You can be replaced with a finger snap!

That day, something inside me snapped. I could no longer live my life being someone else's puppet. I wanted to be in control of my income, my vacations, my hours, and my decisions. I had no idea what I was going to do. I knew I wasn't going to sit on my hands anymore.

You know when you want to buy a new car, you start seeing the same car everywhere? I started looking into online ads about work-from-home opportunities. I discovered a whole world of online marketers who were making my monthly salary in a lazy afternoon using their laptops. I was hooked. I learned I could liberate myself from the chains of my job.

I got online and started looking at different income opportunities. I signed up for a bunch of email newsletters. I started watching videos and trying to learn this online marketing stuff. Honestly, as soon as I entered that world, I found a passion for it. I love everything about being able to do stuff online and somehow create a commission. I find it magical – to be able to stay home all day or travel and have commissions appear in my account.

First, I joined an income opportunity that was very hot at the time. It didn't work out for me, but looking back, I now see all the things I wasn't doing right, so that was on me. Then I got into all kinds of search engine marketing because everybody said traffic was the #1 thing. What you don't realize is that Google is in control here. You're under their umbrella. If they change anything, you don't get a say in their decisions. By the time I finished learning about search engines, all the information I had learned was old news.

I saw no commissions for the first year online. I was going from one opportunity to another to another. Eventually, I somehow ended up on the Warrior Forum. It was the end of the year again. I was going through different threads, and I came across Igor. I started looking at his coaching program, and I saw a whole bunch of people saying he helped them fire their boss. What was cool was the fact that it wasn't any particular type of person. I saw people who looked exactly like me, my age, my background, 30+ years old. I also saw females who were over 50 years old. I also saw kids who were 19 years old. I saw a whole variety of people, and I was like, "Wow! This must be something different, because if it was working for all these people, it might work for me, too." I decided to talk to Igor. I filled out a form and booked a call with his assistant.

We connected a couple of weeks later. (It was a grueling process to get Igor on the phone.) He asked me a lot of questions. He wanted to know who I was and what I was going through. After I answered all his questions, he said he thought he could help me and told me more about his coaching program. He showed me how much he was making, how much his students were making, and what was possible for me.

Honestly, I know what I'm going to say right now is not going to make sense, but it was too good to be true. Igor and his clients were making more in a month than I was making in a whole year. I didn't believe it was possible. It was too much, and out of sheer fear, I did not join.

Let me say if there was a mistake, I have ever made online, that was saying "No" to Igor. That was probably the biggest mistake I've ever made online. I went back to trying all kinds of shiny objects. I wasted another year. I was miserable. I wanted to figure out this online marketing thing so bad.

Exactly a year later, I was on the Warrior Forum again. I was looking for the next $27 product to buy and refund. Another magic trick. Another silver bullet. As I was browsing the threads, I stumbled into the same thread where Igor was talking about his coaching program. Not much had changed with that thread except it grew with more case studies! While I wasted another year trying shiny objects, Igor helped dozens more people start earning money online. I felt so stupid. I reached out to Igor again asking for coaching. It didn't matter to me what he charged or how his coaching program worked. I knew he was going to help me. It had to work for me because it worked for other people.

I signed up, and I did exactly what Igor told me. He told me about how I needed to build a list and showed me how to get started. He explained to me how to get email traffic and what to offer to this traffic. Then he showed me a simple way to write marketing emails. From there, I repeated the process every day. I'd get traffic, build my email list, and send out emails.

In the next three months, I'd experienced an extreme makeover. I couldn't believe how fast things were happening for me. In the first month, I made $1,500. I didn't profit. I made enough sales to cover my advertising expenses. I was reinvesting every dollar back into solo ads. My list was growing fast. Igor said I should play the long game and keep building my email list, so I did. In my second month, I made $4,200. Some of it was profit, but I didn't care. I put everything back into the business. My list was now growing even faster. I was recouping my money almost immediately. In the third month, my online business exploded. I made $17,000 ($7,000 profit), and my email list was 12,000 subscribers strong. By my fourth month, I was bringing in $18,000 net. My highest month that year was $27,000.

Just like Igor promised, I made more in 12 months than I had in the previous 12 years. I have gotten to a point where I can write an email to my list within three minutes, hit "send," and watch commissions come into my account. Last month, I grossed over $140,000 in commissions with my email list of 60,000 subscribers.

The great part is no one knows what I'm doing. No one gets in my face about it. Even my mom doesn't know how I make a living. This year, I bought a brand-new home with all this "internet money" and I know exactly how I'm going to pay off the mortgage ahead of time! Next week, I'm taking my daughter, Karina, to Disneyland in California. I'm not taking my laptop with me. I know money's coming in whether I work or not. This is what freedom is all about. I have no schedule. I wake up when I'm done sleeping. On days I feel like working, I put in a couple of hours into writing emails and creating offers for my email subscribers. Sometimes I do it in the middle of the day. Other times, in the middle of the night. On days when my daughter, Karina, is with me, I don't touch my computer. I don't work. I never wanted to be one of those dads who is either always at work or talks to their kids through their smartphone screen. And it is all thanks to Igor.

David Dekel
Toronto, Canada

The fastest way to get results is to get a mentor. Would you like to be mentored by Igor? Visit www.igor.cx/tools for details

Free List Building Resources

About the author

Igor Kheifets is the world's highest-paid email marketer. Igor specializes in helping average people break the link between their time and their income. He's the founder and CEO of Igor Solo Ads, www.igorsoloads.com, the world's #1 email traffic agency which has helped thousands of people build a wildly profitable email list without any previous experience.

BONUS! Free Traffic Training for List Building Lifestyle Readers

Exclusive workshop with Igor Kheifets shows how to generate 500 buyer leads a day with email marketing. Attend free by visiting www.igor.cx. It is a perfect place to start if you're a beginner.

BONUS! Subscribe to List Building Lifestyle Podcast

Get free list building coaching from Igor on your way to work, in the gym, or when grocery shopping. Subscribe to List Building Lifestyle Show for free tips, tricks, and strategies on making big money with small email lists. Visit www.listbuildinglifestyleshow.com

Would you like to be personally mentored by Igor for $3.23 per day?

Work directly with Igor on your online business. Gain access to his network of partners, collaborators and students. Become a list building insider by joining the World's #1 list building mastermind coaching group at 50% OFF by visiting: www.listbuildinglifestyle.com.

Head over to www.igor.cx/tools for additional tips, tricks and resources to living the List Building Lifestyle!

Internet Marketing Dictionary

404 Error
broken link, incorrect address.

Affiliate marketing
performance-based marketing in which a business rewards one or more affiliates for each visitor or customer brought by the affiliate's own marketing efforts.

Autoresponder
bulk email service which has the capability of automatically following up with leads via email and/or text message.

Affiliate link
a unique link provided to an affiliate marketer to promote the online product or service which is then used to credit commissions to the affiliate.

Bridge page
pre-sell landing page which "warms up" the prospect towards investigating the sales page.

Buy Now button (aka Add-To-Cart button)
the button or link the prospective buyer needs to click to place an order.

Bot traffic
fake traffic which consists of automated scripts and robots (bots) used by scammers who pose to sell legit traffic.

Blacklist
put a person or product on a blacklist.

Business opportunity
a program which allows you to earn money from home without a product of your own.

Back end
all offers presented to the prospect after the front-end offer.

Banned
officially prohibited.

Cookie
a seamless element a website drops on the machine when visiting the website to remember the visitor when he returns.

Call to action
language pattern which encourages the prospect to act or purchase.

Conversion rate
the percentage of users who take a desired action.

Click-Through Rate
metric used to discover the efficiency of one's email campaign measured by dividing total number of email hits by total amount of email opens for that campaign.

Click
a visitor to your website, opt-in page, landing page, or sales page.

Double opt-in
the process of building an email which requires for each opt-in to confirm subscription by clicking a confirmation link in a follow-up email.

Delivery Rate
percentage of emails which land in the subscriber's inbox, measured by your Autoresponder company.

Domain
the address you type into your web browser address bar to visit a website (e.g. Google.com).

Downline
people you recruit into your network marketing organization.

Email Open Rate
metric used to discover the efficiency of one's email campaign measured by dividing total number of opens by total amount of email recipients for that campaign.

Facebook ads
Facebook pay-per-click traffic source.

Freebie
gift or bribe.

Follow Up Email
an email which is sent to the prospective buyer automatically through your email auto responder to follow up with them.

Follow Up Sequence
a sequence of emails which is sent to the prospective buyer automatically through your email auto responder to follow up with them.

Front end
first offer in a sequence of offers in a sales funnel.

Google AdWords
Google's pay-per-click traffic source.

High ticket
high priced.

Info product
information which helps to solve a problem packaged into an easy-to-access digital format and sold for a nominal fee.

Lead/Prospect
a visitor who showed interest in your offer by opting in on your squeeze page.

Link Cloaking
masking your long affiliate link using a cloaking software so it doesn't look like an affiliate link.

List building

the process of building an email list of targeted prospects interested in your product or service.

Low ticket

low priced.

Micro commitment

small commitment which leads to large commitment.

Mobile Friendly

optimized for mobile use.

Opt-In

an action a prospect takes on a squeeze page by entering his/her information (e.g. email address) into a form and clicking "submit."

Opt-In Rate

metric used to discover the efficiency of one's squeeze page/landing page calculated by dividing total number of unique visits to a landing page by total number of opt-ins.

Order form

comprehensive form the client fills out to submit their order, which includes their contact details, credit card information, and billing address.

Opt-in form

web form into which the visitor enters their email address and/or name on the squeeze page.

OTO

one time offer.

Passive income
income received on a regular basis with little effort
required to maintain it.

PPC
short for Pay-Per-Click.

PLR
private label rights.

PPC Traffic
one of the ways to drive traffic to your landing page where
you pay per click generated and not per impression or
action. Pay-Per-Click traffic sources include Facebook Ads,
Solo Ads, Google AdWords.

Pop-Up Traffic
web visitors which originate from a pop-up page.

Pop-Under Traffic
web visitors which originate from a pop-under page.

Raw Click
a visit to a page made multiple times from a single
computer.

Rotator Link
a parent web link which rotates several internal links.

Reseller
broker.

ROI
return on investment.

Squeeze page (aka. Opt-in Page, Landing Page, and Capture Page)
Simple, one-page website designed to get the visitor to share their email address in exchange for a gift or a piece of information.

Sales page
landing page which contains a sales letter and/or sales video which markets the product, service, or opportunity.

Sales Video
a short video which explains the features and the benefits of a product, service, program, or opportunity and encourages the prospect to invest.

Single Opt-In
the process of building an email which requires no confirmation.

Subscriber
Opt-in.

SPAM
unsolicited email.

Scarcity
state of being scarce or in short supply.

Thank You Page
the landing page prospect is being redirected to immediately after they have opted in.

Tracking
software which measures your website performance.

Target Redirect
the page web visitor is redirected to after taking some
sort of action.

Tier 1/Top Tier
Top-quality traffic locations: United States, Canada,
Australia, United Kingdom, and New Zealand.

Takeaway Selling
a psychological trigger that lets the prospect know that
they CAN'T HAVE what you used to offer at this time. The
takeaway is telling them, "Well, if you'd responded to the
letter, we sent you six months ago, you could have
received the $3,000 discount we were offering for all
customers who converted. Because you waited, you now
have to pay the conversion fee of $3,000."

Tire Kicker
time waster, someone who's not serious.

Unique Click
a single, unique visit to a page.

Upline
sponsor.

Unsubscribe
when an email subscriber opts out of receiving emails.

Upsell
a sales technique whereby a seller induces the customer
to purchase more expensive items, upgrades, or other
add-ons to make a more profitable sale.

USP
unique selling proposition.

Whitelist
add to approved contacts.

Webinar
online seminar hosted using a teleconference software.

What To Do Next?

My intention was to help you see and understand what it's like to make six figures and be your own boss by building a large responsive email list. At this point, you're either fired up to learn more or you've learned List Building Lifestyle is not for you. If you don't like the idea of making a lot of money anytime you send out an email, I thank you for investing the time to read this book and I hope our path will cross in the future. If, however, you love the idea of firing your boss using email marketing, I've got some great news for you. This book is just the tip of the iceberg. If you'd like to go deeper into the rabbit hole to find out how I'm generating thousands of leads each and every day without touching my computer, I invite you to attend a free Rapid Automated Traffic workshop I'm hosting at **www.igor.cx**.

Attend this free workshop to find out how to get virtually unlimited traffic to any offer, product or niche. Discover how I bootstrapped my way to generating 4,331,656 email opt in leads without losing money. I'll also share how I recoup 400% more money on my solo ad campaigns.

Oh, and just for attending, you're getting a $3,097 value "ethical bribe" – a 31-day email sequence, you can use to promote affiliate offers to your email list. RSVP your free seat at **www.igor.cx** right now.

<u>Here Are Three More Ways I Can Help You Live The *List Building Lifestyle*</u>:

1. **Subscribe to List Building Lifestyle Podcast.** Get free list building coaching from Igor on your way to work, in the gym, or when grocery shopping. Subscribe to List Building Lifestyle Show for free tips, tricks, and strategies on making big money with small email lists. Visit **www.listbuildinglifestyleshow.com**

2. **Would you like to be personally mentored by Igor for $3.23 per day?** Work directly with Igor on your online business. Gain access to his network of partners, collaborators, and students. Become a list building insider by joining the World's #1 list building mastermind coaching group at 50% OFF by visiting: **www.listbuildinglifestyle.com**

3. **Would you like me to drive traffic and build your email list for you, RISK-FREE?** Instead of trying to figure out traffic generation and list building on your own, let me build your first email list for you. I'll cherry-pick the best prospects, hook you up with a free email auto responder and I'll even help you pick a profitable product to promote to your email subscribers.
Visit **www.igorsoloads.com** for details.

Even More Praise For Igor Kheifets

"I've known Igor for years. Few people understand list building at the level he does."

Kameron George, founder, AWOL Academy

"I've worked closely with Igor to promote my high-ticket program. By the end of the week, Igor referred 47 new $1,997 customers and $93,758 in sales. Igor has some of the most responsive traffic in internet marketing."

Brendan Mace, founder, Project Profit Academy

"Trust me, if you want big numbers, talk to Igor!"

Michael Cheney, founder, 7-Figure Franchise

"I've worked with many traffic experts. Igor operates on another level."

Paulo Barroso, Super-Affiliate

"If you want to build a big, quality list quickly, talk to Igor. He knows more about list building than anyone I know of."

Devon Brown, founder, Easiest Sales System

"Stuff he teaches works. Implementing his advice has dramatically increased my bottom line. Work with Igor. He will change your life."

James Francis, London, United Kingdom

"I started working with Igor when I was down to my last dollar. I got married and was trying to find some success online. Today, I've already made over $200,000 since starting with Igor. Thanks to the stability that comes with having my own online business, I finally decided to start my own family. Work with Igor. He can change your life."

Juan Morales, Panama City, Panama

"I was making $100 a day with my own email list before I started working with Igor. Igor showed me how to take it to $400 a day while taking two months off to travel the country in my motorhome without an internet connection."

Ed Newman, Super-Affiliate

"When the real estate market crashed, I was struggling to recover and eventually decided to try internet marketing. I picked a niche product and started looking for traffic. I was using email solo ads, but they weren't converting. Then I found Igor. Igor took the time to work with me, to ask me questions and to show me what works. He cared. The first ad I ran with Igor brought in $15,000 in sales. Since then, I've been known as the Magnetic Marketer. Thank you for caring and for helping me, Igor!"

Miles Segers, aka "Magnetic Marketer"

"Igor's a perfectionist and a professional. He's a wise head on young shoulders. He's been instrumental at helping us grow our organization."

Albert Koster, Australia

"Internet marketing niche isn't an easy market to make money in consistently the way Igor does. If you want to make money in this market, I can't recommend Igor enough."

Ben Settle, chief editor, Email Players

"Igor's a master at what he does. If you're looking to grow your business online, no one is better than Igor at helping you do that."

Tom Beal, Author, Speaker, Success Coach

"Getting coaching from Igor was one of the best decisions I've made in my life."

James Canzanella, Super-Affiliate

"When Igor talks, I listen. Since I started working with Igor, I've grown a huge email list and have since quit my job, bought a new home, and travel 30 days out of the year. It is all thanks to Igor!"

David Dekel, founder, FunnelX

"Igor's one of the brightest minds in his space."

Keala Kanae, CEO, AWOL Academy

"If you get a chance to work with Igor, take it. Study what he's doing."

Richard Legg, founder, Six-Figure Apprentice

Made in the USA
Lexington, KY
16 September 2019